DEMOTED
PLANET

DEMOTED
PLANET

Katherine Fallon

Finalist for the Charlotte Mew Prize

HEADMISTRESS PRESS

Copyright © 2021 by Katherine Fallon
All rights reserved.

ISBN 978-1-7358236-0-7

This book may not be reproduced, in whole or in part, including illustrations, in any form (beyond that permitted by Sections 107 and 108 of the U.S. Copyright Law and except by reviewers for the public press), without written permission from the publishers.

Cover art: Romaine Brooks, *Peter (A Young English Girl)*, 1923-1924, oil on canvas, Smithsonian American Art Museum, Gift of the artist, 1970.70
Cover & book design by Mary Meriam.

PUBLISHER
Headmistress Press
60 Shipview Lane
Sequim, WA 98382
Telephone: 917-428-8312
Email: headmistresspress@gmail.com
Website: headmistresspress.blogspot.com

For our High Commander, who applied to be
an astronaut on his deathbed.

Contents

CUSP OF CARABELLI	1
VIEWING	2
THE NUTCRACKER, MARZIPAN DANCERS, 1986	3
EARLY ADOPTER	4
ELEGY FOR MY FATHER	5
REVELRY	6
DISCARD	7
THRESHOLD	8
SMART	9
VOYAGER, -BOUND, FATHER	10
PNEUMATIC	11
BLUR	12
OBJECT IMPERMANENCE	13
REFUSE	14
I FORGOT ALL ABOUT THE WEEDING AFTER	15
DARK SIDE OF THE MOON	16
FUNEREAL	17
THE WINTER WE MOVED HERE	18
ON THE ANNIVERSARY OF HIS PASSING	20
OTHERWISE	21
WANDERING STAR	22
REPLICANT	23
About the Author	27
Acknowledgements	29

I'm stepping through the door/
and I'm floating in a most peculiar way/
and the stars look very different today

"Space Oddity," David Bowie

CUSP OF CARABELLI

I dreamt our parents gave a lecture we expected
to be on teeth: Mother with the blue-orange

blow torch and a violent, spinning crucible; Father
with the soft-tongued secret of the Cusp of Carabelli.

But Mother didn't speak and Dad wrote endless code
on the green board. He said, *Now then, doesn't that*

make sense? And we agreed. No one's ever liked
to disappoint him. He clapped his hands and a cloud

of white dust spread through the room. *And that's how
it happens, my little ones,* he said, pointing to his tidy

characters, *that's how and why everything decays.*

VIEWING

Stone father, I did touch you. First your folded hands,
which straightened the frothy lace of my childhood

party dresses, one of many clumsy tendernesses.
Then I kissed your refrigerated forehead and knew,

truly, for the first time, what *unreciprocated* means.
It was and somehow remains your job to teach me lessons.

THE NUTCRACKER, MARZIPAN DANCERS, 1986

We made ourselves small beneath the practice bar
where Mother's toe shoes swept the floor, took in
the dusty smell of tights before curtain. Father's eyes

in the dark hall were wet. He caressed the velvet
arm rests—calluses catching like striking a match
beneath the orchestra's swell—and pointed: she was

That One. We thought that marvelous, as they all
looked the same, like a tray of petit fours. Waiting
for her after the show, we collected shed sequins

from the lobby carpet. He later helped us string them
into necklaces we wore while attempting our own
arabesques, though their facets were lost for facing.

EARLY ADOPTER

On a few occasions, I caught Dad
in the yard with a sledgehammer

or a drill, a saw or a hatchet—
tools he never employed otherwise,

tools I didn't even know he owned—
going after a keyboard that no longer

cared what he wanted, or a bottlefly
green motherboard that had become

a minute silenced city. He had plenty
of material. Each thing he brought home

would inevitably fail or be replaced
by progress. I saw him sweating,

at war. I dodged shrapnel, watched it
glitter in an arc across the sun.

ELEGY FOR MY FATHER

My father and I collided in the downstairs
hallway most nights. We never were able to

sleep. We'd sit at that awful lion-footed
walnut table they were both so proud of,

leaf missing, a perfect circle that could never
again grow larger and, more troubling,

couldn't ever seem to close completely,
gathering crumbs we loosed with butter knives

evenings we sat together as a family, eating.
Those late nights, my father drank whole milk

and talked while I drew my finger awkwardly
along the whorls of the wood, his face too much

like someone I knew to look right into.
There wasn't much to say then. He was forty

and I was curling my hair daily until
the singed waft of it filled the bathroom.

Still, we kept vigil for hours without lighting
the room. The refrigerator opened, closed,

opening, closing. Just a portal we could have
climbed through, together but one by one.

REVELRY

I watched from my window while tall,
thin men danced through the trash fire

in our backyard, hollering as they climbed
up and down the flaming backsteps

they'd just replaced. What filth I heard,
their vowels all syrup, their feet glowing

with flame. Beers in hand, they scuffed
against the grass to put themselves out.

I searched and found my father in shadow,
present but hardly a man if this is what

makes them. Next day, I woke to the quiet
hiss of the garden hose. He was soaking

the charred earth, afraid the smolder
had burned all night without him.

DISCARD

He worked with brushes, a loupe,
with fire and bone-breaking force.

Following him from Bunsen burner
to hurtling crucible, I witnessed

the separation of clement from dross,
heard the corn husk rustle of insects

who'd climbed into the slag to hide
and died from heat. I chose a piece

to keep, thin as a petal and tarnished
as alloy, interpreted it like forcing

clouds into shapes from the limits
of the ground: a whale, a crown,

an open mouth. What had I learned,
save the shapes excess takes?

THRESHOLD

Early, in our separate rooms,
        we were wrong to believe
in a middling, an I, the illusion
        of self within the chimera
of family. When he lifted our doors
        from their hinges, he punished us
not only with being seen, but with
        admitting, at last, to influence.
Being mirrors, it was impossible
        to be children. Impossible, too,
to mature. I come to you now,
        sister, seeking all I once
renounced: mainly, open doors,
        though finally, I'd rather
no doors at all—
        Sister, I remain—

SMART

Spitting pan, tapped eggshell, I made
breakfast for her and as she recalled

ovoid marks from his favorite weapon,
my wooden spoon stayed in a drawer.

At times he hit so hard he broke handles.
I have no frame of reference. Once

while brushing our teeth, my sister
and I were surprised by the yard stick's

bite and the bruises behind our knees
fit together like two parts of one

shattered thing. Transgression long
forgotten, all that's left is our father's

height, diminished, and his choking
tenderness, asking our forgiveness.

VOYAGER, -BOUND, FATHER

In the dark room of a difficult boyhood, sick
with television glow, you saw them stab the moon

through with a flag and never forgot. Believing
ever since in other, surely better worlds, you'd rather

be up there with anti-gravity, your old bones buoyed,
seeming never to have met. There's no space in space

and so no way to hold you, and when you do let go,
you'll sink down low, rising, too, like a dreamy cream top,

milk galaxy wallpaper behind you. I'd give you away—
a way up—if I could. Already, you might as well be

the silence of Voyager's orbit, the golden record itself:
far-flung message, eternally unheard.

PNEUMATIC

      Wanamaker Grand Court Organ, Philadelphia, PA

The year your lungs stopped,
I hoofed scaffolds inside an organ

with twenty-nine thousand pipes—
some small as straws, others

large as ponies, all dull as unlit
closets. The wheeze of waiting

was so human I hardly noticed it
until at last I came to know

the tremolo of potential, both
before the force and after,

the lingering ghost song.
Before long, your sounds grew

fewer and fewer and we listened,
ear to chest, for any interior hum.

I thought I knew but I did not,
could not know labor until I saw it.

BLUR

We all in turn caught on to the Darth Vader
click-and-exhale of the oxygen concentrator,

which went from rolling suitcase to missile-sized
the night you refused treatment and sunk truly

into hospice. Leah was the last of us to understand
the origin of the sound, having traveled from

so far away, but she woke me—
surrounded by longnecks and loose shake—

on the morning you passed. I never thought
I had more time, just didn't know that you would

become this: a hazy, screen-like sheath between
myself and the world, like Vaseline on glass,

lack of focus proof that I loved you enough.

OBJECT IMPERMANENCE

The nurse appeared to bathe him during the hour
my mother was gone for groceries. Like the child

he was re-becoming, he hid behind me. No other
woman had ever seen him naked, but the nurse,

kind as she was, wouldn't wait. He placed himself
in her hands, allowed her to prop him mannequin-

like against Travertine, wipe clean his retired sex,
the thinning white pelt of his chest. Soon after,

Mother returned with milk to find him scrubbed
and dazed. He hadn't missed her in so long.

REFUSE

The last day he was upright, I helped my sister
heave his weight. He didn't make it to the toilet—

hadn't in weeks—but he insisted. The horrid,
empty smell was wholly new and broke me.

He hadn't eaten for days. What could be left
to void? I gagged as it seeped down his bird leg,

then left my sister to the mess. He was still alert
enough to know that I had turned my back

and he was hurt, though hurting worse in other ways,
he never mentioned it, taking to bed for good

shortly after, leaving me to regret what everyone
regrets after death: the way things were when

there was still a chance of fixing things;
the fact that no one tried.

I FORGOT ALL ABOUT WEEDING AFTER

I watched two men pull the sheath—
folded like napkins in all the places

I fear, for class, I don't belong—
over your greying face. With heavy

rains since, the yard's gone wildly
lush. As you were seeing things

in cellophane air, you called me
radiant, like I was Zuckerman's

famous pig. Of all the things
you forgot, you never didn't know

who I was. Now is the time of dirt
sinking down inside its bed,

giving way to pioneer species,
which would flower if we let them.

DARK SIDE OF THE MOON

Everyone could see your Pink Floyd t-shirt,
but not what we nestled below the half-shut
lid without the undertaker's knowing:

full ounce of quality weed and a teddy bear
so loved the stuffing had dissolved, leaving
a floppy, pilled exoskeleton behind. Your skin,

however it could, looked like skin. Eyes
glued shut I'm sure but it looked more like sleep
than—   I had waited you out until you

expired, as you were meant to, and I wept,
as I was meant to. Days passed, and I understood
grief to be a room I'd entered, with provisions.

FUNEREAL

After the funeral, gaudy pageantry:
sprays and vases of roses, gladiolas,

and bells of Ireland, braided together
like parade floats, lining the halls

of the house, quiet since the machines
had been turned off. Most arrangements

festered in water or went paper-dry
on plastic boning, but the lilies persisted

in velvet soil, tied with ribbon,
their need a dogged weight I wore

like regalia. Blooming, they took up
all the space you'd left in your wake.

THE WINTER WE MOVED HERE

we covered my father's funeral lily

to save it   from frost burn

and its leaves bent so low

beneath the white sheet they became

a body   at rest

to be headed off at dawn

that spring a man in a semi failed to stop

        at the sight of brake lights

and five nursing students   all women

some too young to drink   were killed

on their way to clinicals

on the raw shoulder as many crosses

                    sprang up   clad in bleached

    lab coats   which   in the gales

    of passing traffic

                            billowed

                    pillowed

                                        snapped.

ON THE ANNIVERSARY OF HIS PASSING

I look through years of home videos in hopes
of finding my father, who was always behind

the camera. I hear him in each take but see him
only once, decorating the tree. I am four. I ask

to be lifted to an out-of-reach bough, and when
he holds out his hand for me, I barrel toward him,

falling on my face at his feet. Unformed, I look up
to him, wait to be told wordlessly whether to cry.

He helps me stand, checks for injury, admonishes:
you have got to watch where you are going.

OTHERWISE

I think of the fracture, how for months
my wife had to lift me by the stretch-
marked hips over the lip of the bathtub
and out again by the armpits, chafed
like road rash. The both of us found
my infirmity sexy—I let her put her face
wherever—until it persisted.

I bruised her shins with my cast in sleep.

For years, my mother had to control
my father's oxygen. He gradually curled up
like a cocktail shrimp, inhaler wobbling
violently in his grip. But I remember
otherwise, too: whistling in the bathroom,
dressed for parties with paper invitations.
I'd kill to keep it from happening.

The year of our suicide draws nearer.

WANDERING STAR

Father, you are finally the ghost elephant,
now the vacant boat, now the spot on the wall

where a portrait used to hang, brighter
than its surrounds, footprint of a vanishing.

You are the cockless dawn, the cloudless
sky, the draught-blighted farmland

of the Midwest. Deep in earth though not
of Earth at all, you are black-hole material:

demoted planet, imploded star, I wake
because you taught me of landings.

REPLICANT

I.

In my latest dream, your chest rose and fell
while we counted the seconds between breaths
with a literal stopwatch, which made it seem
real because that is what made your death real
years ago: the counting kept on, and you didn't.

II.

So you vacated again and I counted my own breath,
tracing it from gaping mouth to cold, broke-open
breastbone to stomach, that putrid, mutinous lagoon.

Then, what ought to have alerted me to falsehood:
your belly inflated again, your sternum rose
and you fought the rails of your coffin, sat upright,

a jack-in-the-box escaping the horror dream
I could not—though was I trying?

III.

You never did open your eyes, but I knew the panic
was not mindless, not the thrashing of the cliché
undead. You were with me again, flesh and bone,

and you were suffering. Your blood bubbled
like an untended pot, pooling at the ears.

You bruised like the skin of an overripe pear.

IV.

I could not hold you down,
momentarily restored
to the bear-paw strength
of the times you built fires
and took your own damn self

to the bathroom. Back when
your haunches looked like
haunches, not chair legs,
inside your jeans. Back
when you wore jeans.

I quit trying. At last,
you died again, which was
the third time but felt like
the first. And the twelfth.
Also the forty-fourth.

V.

So much is left of you, but none of it human.

About the Author

Katherine Fallon attended Bryn Mawr and Sarah Lawrence Colleges and is the author of *The Toothmakers' Daughters* (Finishing Line Press, 2018). Her work has appeared in *AGNI, Colorado Review, Juked, Meridian, Passages North, Foundry,* and *Best New Poets 2019,* among others. She is Poetry Editor at *MAYDAY Magazine,* and a reader for *[PANK].* She lives above the gnat line in South Georgia with her favorite human, who helps her zip her dresses.

Acknowledgments

Apple Valley Review: "ELEGY FOR MY FATHER"

Bear Review: "VOYAGER, -BOUND, FATHER" and "WANDERING STAR"

Bookends Review: "REFUSE"

Eunoia Review: "BLUR"

Innisfree Poetry Journal: "CUSP OF CARABELLI" (as "LETTER TO MY SISTER")

Natural Bridge: "FUNEREAL"

Parentheses Journal: "THRESHOLD"

Plainsongs: "OBJECT IMPERMANENCE" (as "BEGINNINGS")

Rust + Moth: "DARK SIDE OF THE MOON"

The Lake: "THE WINTER WE MOVED HERE"

The Shore: "EARLY ADOPTER" & "REVELRY"

"WANDERING STAR" uses Jean Valentine's "Ghost Elephants," and "vacant boat" from Li Young Lee's "Black Petal."

Headmistress Press Books

Demoted Planet - Katherine Fallon
Earlier Households - Bonnie J. Morris
The Things We Bring with Us: Travel Poems - S.G. Huerta
The Water Between Us - Gillian Ebersole
Discomfort - Sarah Caulfield
The History of a Voice - Jessica Jopp
I Wish My Father - Lesléa Newman
Tender Age - Luiza Flynn-Goodlett
Low-water's Edge - Jean A. Kingsley
Routine Bloodwork - Colleen McKee
Queer Hagiographies - Audra Puchalski
Why I Never Finished My Dissertation - Laura Foley
The Princess of Pain - Carolyn Gage & Sudie Rakusin
Seed - Janice Gould
Riding with Anne Sexton - Jen Rouse
Spoiled Meat - Nicole Santalucia
Cake - Jen Rouse
The Salt and the Song - Virginia Petrucci
mad girl's crush tweet - summer jade leavitt
Saturn coming out of its Retrograde - Briana Roldan
i am this girl - gina marie bernard
Week/End - Sarah Duncan
My Girl's Green Jacket - Mary Meriam
Nuts in Nutland - Mary Meriam & Hannah Barrett
Lovely - Lesléa Newman
Teeth & Teeth - Robin Reagler
How Distant the City - Freesia McKee
Shopgirls - Marissa Higgins
Riddle - Diane Fortney
When She Woke She Was an Open Field - Hilary Brown

A Crown of Violets - Renée Vivien tr. Samantha Pious
Fireworks in the Graveyard - Joy Ladin
Social Dance - Carolyn Boll
The Force of Gratitude - Janice Gould
Spine - Sarah Caulfield
I Wore the Only Garden I've Ever Grown - Kathryn Leland
Diatribe from the Library - Farrell Greenwald Brenner
Blind Girl Grunt - Constance Merritt
Acid and Tender - Jen Rouse
Beautiful Machinery - Wendy DeGroat
Odd Mercy - Gail Thomas
The Great Scissor Hunt - Jessica K. Hylton
A Bracelet of Honeybees - Lynn Strongin
Whirlwind @ Lesbos - Risa Denenberg
The Body's Alphabet - Ann Tweedy
First name Barbie last name Doll - Maureen Bocka
Heaven to Me - Abe Louise Young
Sticky - Carter Steinmann
Tiger Laughs When You Push - Ruth Lehrer
Night Ringing - Laura Foley
Paper Cranes - Dinah Dietrich
On Loving a Saudi Girl - Carina Yun
The Burn Poems - Lynn Strongin
I Carry My Mother - Lesléa Newman
Distant Music - Joan Annsfire
The Awful Suicidal Swans - Flower Conroy
Joy Street - Laura Foley
Chiaroscuro Kisses - G.L. Morrison
The Lillian Trilogy - Mary Meriam
Lady of the Moon - Amy Lowell, Lillian Faderman, Mary Meriam
Irresistible Sonnets - ed. Mary Meriam
Lavender Review - ed. Mary Meriam

www.ingramcontent.com/pod-product-compliance
Lightning Source LLC
Chambersburg PA
CBHW060224050426
42446CB00013B/3163